TOGO:
Brave Dog of Alaska

Written by Lisa Kuehl

Illustrations by Vitaly Dudarenko

ISBN: 9781670388919 (paperback)

This book is dedicated to Prince, Dixie, Jack, Balto, Togo, Scotty, Cub, Jet, Bear, and all the dogs and drivers who risked their lives to save the people of Nome, Alaska in 1925. It is also dedicated to those who carry on the Iditarod tradition today in their memory.

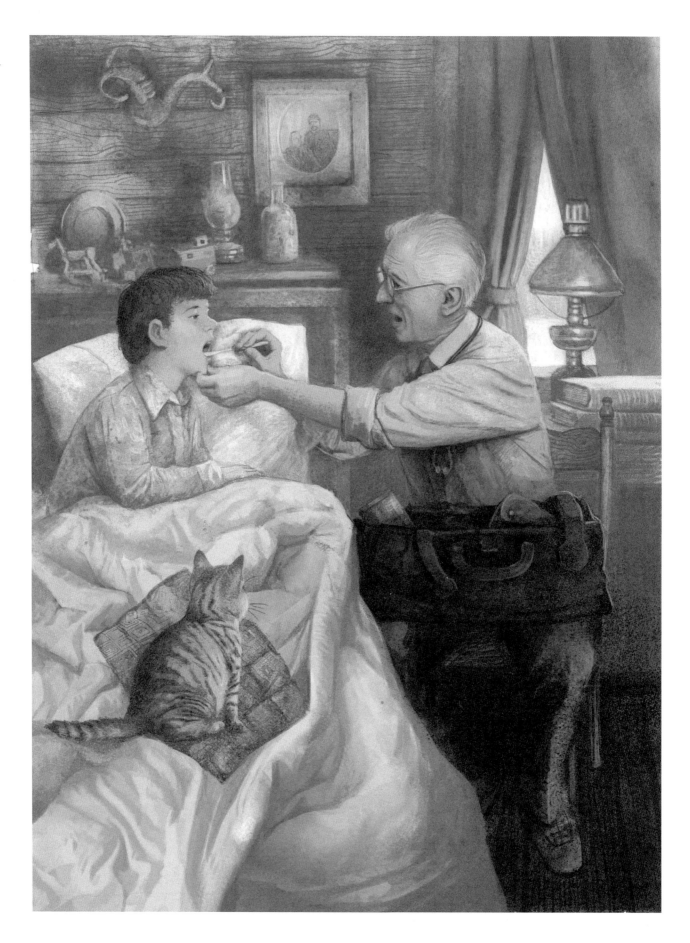

Dr. Welch was sitting up late by the light of his lamp watching over his newest young patient. It was the typical symptoms: it started with a sore throat, and breathing became more and more difficult. It was diphtheria, and in 1925, the vaccine was extremely scarce. There was an anti-toxin serum available, but the batch Dr. Welch had was outdated and wasn't working. There wasn't much left to share of it in the little town of Nome, Alaska, a remote coastal town in the northern territory. The number of cases was growing each day. A little boy had perished the week before.

Dr. Welch sent telegrams back to the lower forty-eight United States for help. There was argument over which was the best way to get the anti-toxin to the village of Nome. Would ship be fastest? Ice was settling in the area and a boat could be stranded. Travel through Alaska by airplane in those days could be very dangerous. Dog sleds delivered the mail, and the drivers, known as "mushers" were strong and capable in the snow. Could a team of dog sleds carry the antitoxin to Nome safely? Temperatures reached to minus 62 degrees Fahrenheit, with wind chills potentially dropping to minus 80 degrees Fahrenheit below zero.

ARCTIC CIRCLE

ALASKA

Nome

Norton Sound

Nenana

Yukon River

Kuskokwim River

Cook Inlet

Seward

It was decided that the dog sled would be the most effective way to get the first batch of anti-toxin serum to the town of Nome. A train would bring the first batch to Nenana, Alaska by train. A total of twenty dog sled drivers and teams were called upon to pass the serum across Alaska from Nenana to Nome, through blizzard, across the dangerous ice covered waters of the Norton Sound, and across extremely rough land that would challenge the strongest and toughest.

Leonard Seppala and his lead dog Togo stood at the brink of the Norton Sound, in the cold white of winter, watching and listening to the ice. The Norton Sound is a large body of water on the shore of Alaska. When it is frozen, it provides a shortcut so that crossing the interior land can be avoided and time is saved. Crossing the iced-over Sound shortens the length of trail, but it certainly has its dangers. Cracks can develop and break the ice up into floes that could carry you out to sea. Just falling through could happen if the ice was too thin. Seppala was deciding whether to travel across the ice or go around the Norton Sound. Traveling across the ice would shorten his travel by a whole day. Seppala had another reason to get to Nome – his little girl Sigrid was there. He did not know if she had been struck by diphtheria or not.

When Togo was a young pup he was very sick with a swollen throat. Seppala's wife spent hours with him in her arms, nursed him back to health. He didn't seem like a very strong, healthy dog.

As Togo grew up, he didn't seem like he would make a good sled dog. Seppala had a difficult time controlling him. It didn't seem like he could behave. Seppala decided that he would not use him as a sled dog, and sold him to a woman. But, Togo broke through a window and ran all the way back to Seppala. Seppala decided that, because of his strong loyalty, Togo deserved to stay with him. Soon, Seppala realized that Togo didn't make a good sled dog – he made an excellent *lead* sled dog.

But today, Togo raised his nose to the air, also listening, and smelling. A dog's ears are sensitive to the cracking and moving sounds that ice can make. Many a dog has stopped in its tracks despite its master's commands to move forward, proving that they can be capable of detecting dangerous ice.

Seppala raced across the Norton Sound carefully watching and listening to the ice for cracking. The trip went well, the ice was safe, and the wind was even at their backs, giving them more power. But, when he reached the other side, a man told him that the route had been changed and he would have to travel back across the Sound to meet the man who would drop the serum off to him. This nearly doubled the amount of miles Seppala and his dogs had to travel! Not only that, but the wind and weather were turning bad, making travel on the ice much more dangerous. Once, Togo had saved Seppala and the team when they were trapped on an ice floe. Togo had risked his life by jumping into the water and pulling a line that brought Seppala to safety. On this day, no other team on the serum run to Nome covered more miles than did Seppala and his brave dog Togo.

When Seppala, Togo and the team finally reached the other side of the Sound, they found Charlie Olsen, the next driver to carry the serum on to Nome. Olsen's team would then carry the serum to Gunnar Kaasen, whose lead dog was Balto. There was one more team before they arrived to Nome, but when Kaasen and Balto arrived at the next stop, the roadhouse was dark and everyone was asleep. Kaasen made the decision to keep on going to Nome to save time. Also, a blizzard was coming which could grow worse with more time. Kaasen and Balto traveled through a blizzard in some of the most difficult and challenging terrain of the serum run.

When Kaasen and Balto arrived in Nome they were met with a welcoming crowd. The medicine had been unharmed, and not one glass ampule had broken. Everyone that received the medicine recovered. Soon a second shipment with even more medicine would be arriving from Seattle, Washington.

Balto and Kaasen became very famous because they were the last team to come into the town of Nome. Balto even had a statue erected for him. Seppala was heartbroken for Togo that he did not receive such recognition, because he had traveled so many more miles than any other dog, even in minus -62 F degree weather.

But history shows that both Togo and Balto, and their drivers were very brave, hardy, and caring, as were all the other men and dogs on the serum run, and all deserved much credit for saving the town of Nome from devastation and tragedy. Togo and Seppala did have a share of fame throughout the United States as well and became very popular. Togo is preserved to this day in a museum in Alaska.

Dog sledding in the United States ceased in the 1960's, but the culture and practice of dog sledding is carried on today in the Iditarod, an annual race in Alaska that still honors the bravery of the men and dogs who successfully carried the anti-toxin serum to Nome.

Friends, it is important to remember that everyone counts. When we work together, it doesn't matter who gets all the fame. What matters is that many lives were saved in a little Alaskan town in the harsh winter of 1925.

Bibliography

Salisbury, Gay and Laney *The Cruelest Miles: The Heroic Story of Dogs and Men in a Race Against an Epidemic.* New York City : W.W. Norton and Company, 2005.

Standiford, Natalie *The Bravest Dog Ever:* The True Story of Balto. Manhattan: Random House, 2003.

About the Author

Lisa Kuehl is a former school teacher living in beautiful Washington State. She enjoys skiing, hiking and camping with her husband, and caring for her two cats and one rabbit.

Her other works include:
Kate Shelley: Heroine of Boone, Iowa
The Magic Brush, a Chinese folktale

About the Illustrator

Vitaly Dudarenko studied at the Minsk Art School in the Belarusian Academy of Arts. He has created illustrations for over 200 books and magazines, and has participated in many international competitions and exhibitions. In 2014, he was awarded the Vasil Vitki medal for his illustrations for the children's magazine, Vyasekla.

Made in the USA
Monee, IL
26 December 2019